Oakland A's

Oakland A's

Photographs by Michael Zagaris
Profiles by John Hickey

Chronicle Books • San Francisco

Photography © 1991 by Michael Zagaris.

Photo credits for A's Past, pages 12–21:
Charlie Finley, page 19, and Bert Campaneris, page 18, reprinted courtesy of UPI/Bettmann. Jim "Catfish" Hunter, page 20, reprinted courtesy of *Oakland Tribune*. Joe Rudi, page 19, reprinted courtesy of AP/Wide World Photos. Sal Bando, page 20, courtesy of *San Francisco Chronicle*. Billy Martin, page 20, and Reggie Jackson, page 21, by Michael Zagaris. All other photographs pages 12–21 reprinted courtesy of National Baseball Library, Cooperstown, New York.

® is the registered logo of the Oakland Athletics. The A's Elephant on page 9 is the official uniform patch and is a trademark ™ of the Oakland Athletics.

Printed in Hong Kong.

Library of Congress Cataloging-in-Publication Data
Hickey, John, 1950–
    Oakland A's / photographs by Michael Zagaris; profiles by John Hickey.
        p.   cm.
    ISBN 0-87701-892-8
    1. Oakland Athletics (Baseball team)—History.
2. Oakland Athletics (Baseball team)—History—Pictorial works.   I. Zagaris, Michael.   II. Title
GV875.O24H53   1991
796.357'64'0979466—dc20   90-26309
                                                                        CIP

Book and cover design: Nielsen O'Brien

Distributed in Canada by Raincoast Books,
112 East Third Avenue, Vancouver, B.C. V5T 1C8

10 9 8 7 6 5 4 3 2 1

Chronicle Books
275 Fifth Street
San Francisco, CA 94103

Page 1: Game 1 of the 1989 World Series at the Oakland Coliseum.

Page 2: A's mob Rick Honeycutt after sweeping 1990 American League Championship Series against the Boston Red Sox.

Page 5: A's dugout greets Rickey Henderson after a home run in Toronto in the fourth game of the 1989 ALCS.

Page 7: October 8, 1989, SkyDome, Toronto. Mark McGwire celebrates A's win over Toronto in the ALCS.

To Kristin and Ari for always being there.
To the Haas family for their direction, and to Sandy Alderson and Tony La Russa for their inspiration and leadership.

ACKNOWLEDGMENTS

Without the help and cooperation of many people this book would never have reached fruition. In no particular order, I'd like to thank the following: Tak Kuno, my lab man at The Photo-Lab, for his work with my black-and-white film; Hugh, Arsinio and Touchdown Tommy at the New Lab, for lending their magic to all our chromes; and Frank and Mike at Imperial Color Labs for peerless prints. Thanks also to the A's front office staff. Most of these people have gone out of their way to assist me over the last ten years. Each and every person in our front office contributes, and they are *all* important, but I'll start with Andy Dolich, in the business operations end of the organization. I have four other bosses: Jay Alves, our director of information, who keeps me hopping with his wit and baseball expertise; Rob Kelly, my mentor in publications; and Kathy Jacobson and Doreen Alves from our media relations department. Special appreciation to Sandy Alderson, not only for his making blockbuster deals but also for that futuristic style so unlike most baseball people, and to Bill Rigney, for his presence alone, as well as his great love for the game and his incredible memory.

    More thanks to Sharon Kelly, Carmen Tiritilli, Sally Lorette, Suzanne Davis, Pam Pitts, Kathy DeLima, Mickey Morabito (our fearless director of team travel), Kevin Kahn, Matt Strelo, Darold Cox, Steve Page, Alan Ledford, and Dave Binzer. In the clubhouse, thanks to the legend, Frank Ciensczyk, the equipment manager since the team moved here in 1968; he has truly seen it all, and what he missed, his assistants Jimmy Sasaki and Angel have seen; to Mike Thalblum, Bobby "The Pen" Miller, Steve Vucinich, Barry Weinberg, Larry Davis, Mark Razum, Lon Simmons, Bill King, and Ray Fosse.

    Thanks to my editor at Chronicle Books, Jay Schaefer, for his patience and persistence and for convincing me this could work, and to Sharilyn Hovind, for transcribing and listening to story after story; to designers Cathleen O'Brien and Lucy Nielsen, whose eyes, suggestions, and graphic alchemy crafted this into much more than a scrapbook; and to Keith Rendel, my assistant and spiritual baseball advisor over the years. Special thanks to my wife, Kristin, for her patience during the long season, for keeping meals warm during extra-inning games, for her sense of humor during losing streaks, and for reminding me by her presence of what is really important in life; and to my son, Ari, thank you for the treasure of allowing me to rediscover the joy of baseball, with you and through you.

Contents

Preface

By Michael Zagaris

For most of us who grew up on the West Coast in the years immediately after World War II our first exposure to Major League baseball was on television. Dizzy Dean and Buddy Blattner broadcast the Game-of-the-Week every Saturday. During the week we listened to Van Patrick on Mutual Radio doing re-creations of the Major League Game-of-the-Day. The broadcasts on radio and television, along with our baseball cards and pulp magazines, were as close as we got to the Big Leagues. In Stockton, California, there was the California League with the Stockton Ports. It was class-C ball and we loved it. I can still smell the cigar and pipe smoke mixed with the aroma of stale popcorn and freshly mown grass at Billy Hebert Field. A really big excursion meant an hour-and-a-half ride to Seals Stadium to see the Seals play the Oakland Oaks, Hollywood Stars (with my two favorites, Carlos Bernier and Bobby Bragan), L.A. Angels, or Portland Beavers, among other teams.

In the early and mid-1950s, the New York Yankees and Brooklyn Dodgers dominated play, so when the Dodgers and the New York Giants moved West in 1958 it was a dream come true. That first year in Seals Stadium was almost beyond belief. The stadium was a small, intimate park, the kind you rarely see anymore, and it seemed to us you could almost reach out and touch the players. And what players they were: Hank Aaron, Willie Mays, Duke Snider, Robin Roberts, Warren Spahn, Stan "The Man" Musial, Frank Robinson, The Big Klu, and *my* favorite—the Pirates' Roberto Clemente.

My brother Bruce and I began hanging out in the lobby of the Sheraton-Palace Hotel on Market Street in San Francisco. In those days the hotel lobbies weren't jammed with baseball-card-clutching autograph seekers. You could actually go up to most of the players, greet them, and talk baseball. Occasionally, guys like Willie and Tommy Davis of the Dodgers would invite you up to their rooms to continue talking and sometimes even to listen to records. Those were the days when to kill time on the road, guys like Juan Marichal and the Alou brothers would head down to 42nd Street in New York to catch part of a triple-feature

Western before grabbing a cab to the Polo Grounds for a night game with the hapless Mets . . . or so they said. For athletes—for all of us—it was a different time.

In the spring of 1961, my sophomore year in high school, John Kennedy was emerging from the debacle of the Bay of Pigs. Mantle and Maris were mounting an assault on Babe Ruth's home-run record, the San Francisco Giants were battling the Reds, and the Dodgers and the Kansas City Athletics were mired in the cellar of the American League. The entire country was reveling in prosperity, baseball was king, and kids collected baseball cards because they symbolized dreams, not investments. The country was nearing the end of a never-to-be-repeated era. Within a short time an assassin's bullet in Dallas changed everything in America. Not just politically, culturally, and spiritually but also for the sporting scene as well.

Baseball had dominated sports in this country since the turn of the century, though it had been losing ground to football since the mid-1950s. In 1957, the sudden death championship game between the Baltimore Colts and the New York Giants proved to be a watershed. Pro football came of age and soon came to represent the Changing American Psyche. First Dallas, then the English invasion with the Beatles and Rolling Stones, and finally Vietnam signaled a radical change in the mood and tempo of the country. Baseball harkened back to a slower, quieter, more innocent time. With America undergoing dramatic social upheavals, the speed, violence, and spectacle of football seemed to reflect life in this country in the 1960s, 1970s, and early 1980s.

Like many others in my generation, I was caught up in the change. Baseball hadn't changed, but I had. Involved in the music scene and the tumultuous political and cultural upheavals, I rarely went to a ball game, and, when I did, the feeling I brought to the ballpark was different. When I'd occasionally tune in a game on TV, I saw new cylinder-shaped stadiums with plastic grass and guys that slapped down on the ball and ran like greyhounds. *This* is *baseball*? I didn't think so. I opted for the Stones, the Who, Led Zepplin, the Quicksilver Messenger Service.

Going out on tour to photograph bands, shooting fashion, and photographing the San Francisco 49ers occupied most of my time.

Toward the end of the 1980 baseball season Charles Finley sold the Athletics (who had moved to Oakland from Kansas City in 1968) to the Haas family. The A's had dominated baseball in the early 1970s with a collection of gashouse gang types that swept through the American League—and the Reds, Mets, and Dodgers in 1972–1974. The Athletics were legends everyplace but home, where they drew sparse crowds. Then, with the advent of free agency, Finley dismantled his team rather than pay big money. Soon you could find more people at Bill Graham's Fillmore West on a Tuesday night than at any A's game on a weekend. The press had the club ticketed to move to Denver. Finley seemed tired and bored. After decimating one of the great and colorful dynasties, he was ready to cash out and return to the Midwest. Walter A. Haas, Jr., always civic minded, stepped in, purchasing the club in the late fall of 1980 and appointing his son, Wally, and son-in-law, Roy Eisenhardt, to run the ball club. The Bay Area breathed a sigh of relief. The day after Christmas I received a call from a friend of mine who knew Wally Haas. Shortly after the New Year I found myself in the cramped new office of Andy Dolich. Andy, who had just come aboard the A's, was from the Washington, D.C., area and, like Wally and Roy, was young, vibrant, and enthusiastic. Forceful and positive, he foresaw a turn-around both for the franchise and for baseball. After the interview I remember leaving with a feeling of exhilaration. The A's charged out of the blocks quickly in 1981, winning their first 11 games. "Billy Ball" was in full swing, ignited by a youthful Rickey Henderson on the base paths, the best sound system, and the finest baseball atmosphere in the country. The fans flocked to the Coliseum. The A's held on to win the West but lost to the Yankees in the play-offs. But you could feel the change at the Coliseum. Once dubbed "The Oakland Mausoleum" because of its depressing atmosphere, it now rocked to new music, crowd noise, and a truly festive feel. The magic was in the air.

The team stumbled for the next few years, falling into

the cellar in late June 1986. At that point, Wally Haas and Sandy Alderson (the general manager) convinced recently deposed Chicago White Sox manager Tony La Russa to take the reins, and the turn-around began. The emergence of homegrown talent like Jose Canseco, Mark McGwire, Walt Weiss, and Terry Steinbach, and the addition of veterans like Dennis Eckersley, Dave Stewart, Bob Welch, and Dave Henderson have brought the Athletics back to a position of dominance in the baseball world. They have drawn over two million fans for each of the last three seasons—this from a franchise that drew 306,000 for the entire year in 1979.

This book concentrates on the Haas years of the Oakland Athletics, with particular emphasis on the last three seasons (1988–1990). I've tried to capture the team not only in action on the field but also in the clubhouse and dugout. Without the patience and trust of Tony La Russa and every one of the players and clubhouse personnel, this would have been impossible. There were times when it was difficult for them, but the result is the fans' reward. The game action is in color while the clubhouse and much of the dugout is in black and white—because it feels black and white.

I'd like to give extra special thanks to Walter, Jr., and Wally, not only for keeping the Athletics in Oakland but also for putting up the money, the energy, and the chutzpah to turn the entire operation around. And thanks Tony "The Load" La Russa. When the skipper arrived with "Dunc" in July 1986, the turn-around began in earnest. The rest is history—and the best is yet to come.

Introduction

By John Hickey

There is a branch of logic peculiar to baseball that says winning a baseball division title is the hardest single feat in all of team sports. A division title is the best barometer of a team's consistent greatness. The World Series, seven games at best, can be won in a streak, but a division title can only be won in a grind—six months of almost daily combat, 162 games from start to finish.

Given that logic, the Oakland A's, winners of the American League West—the toughest division in baseball—for three straight years starting in 1988, have proven their greatness.

Even so, baseball's dinner course has long been the World Series. The A's came to the main meal three times, only to be forced to endure humble sandwich—losses in the World Series in 1988 and 1990 wrapped around a World Series win in 1989. The eventful 1989 victory over the San Francisco Giants is mixed with the painful losses to the Los Angeles Dodgers in 1988 and the Cincinnati Reds in 1990.

But the A's World Series defeats should be tempered by the realization that Oakland remains baseball's premiere franchise. When major league teams attempt to structure themselves for the long term, Oakland—not Cincinnati,

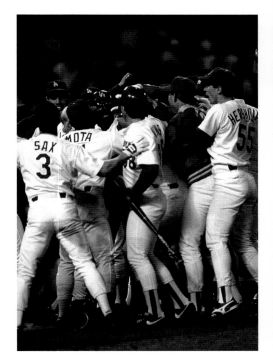

not Los Angeles—is still the model.

Oakland is the team that led the major leagues in victories in each of the last three years. Only 10 other teams since the turn of the century have owned such a stranglehold on the sport.

Oakland is the team that has produced the first pitcher since the 1970s with four straight 20-win seasons—Dave Stewart. It is the team that produced the first pitcher since the popularization of five-man pitching rotations to win more than 25 games—Bob Welch, who won 27 in 1990. It has produced three straight American League team earned run average champions. It has produced a Manager of the Year—Tony La Russa in 1988. It has produced baseball's first 40-40 man—Jose Canseco, who stole 40 bases and hit 42 home runs en route to the MVP award in 1988. It has produced three straight Rookies of the Year—Canseco (1986), Mark McGwire (1987) and Walt Weiss (1988).

Moreover, it has produced teams with heart and a burning desire to succeed. In 1989, the A's achieved victory with Canseco missing more than half a season, with bullpen closer Dennis Eckersley missing 40 games and with shortstop Weiss sidelined for 10 weeks. A year later, it was more of the same. Oakland persevered through the loss of center fielder Dave Henderson and Weiss down the stretch, and with Canseco playing in a much limited capacity due to back and finger injuries.

Still the wins kept coming. And coming. And coming, allowing the A's to lay their claim to being baseball's best.

ABOVE, LEFT: Kirk Gibson receives a tumultuous greeting after his first-game home run starts the Dodgers on their way to an improbable World Series victory, 1988.
ABOVE: Oakland Athletics celebrate sweeping the Giants in the 1989 World Series. PAGE 8: Dave Stewart stares out at the field in the bottom of the first inning, after Cincinnati takes a 2-0 lead in Game 1 of the 1990 World Series.

Tony La Russa

A substantial portion of the missing pieces to the Oakland puzzle were filled in when the A's hired Tony La Russa just 10 days after he'd been fired as manager of the Chicago White Sox in June 1986.

After the traumatic end to his six-year Chicago sojourn, La Russa had planned to take some time off and move back to his Florida home. He, his wife, Elaine, and their two daughters planned to take their first-ever summer vacation together. Instead, he was convinced by Oakland General Manager Sandy Alderson to take the reins of a mediocre Oakland team.

Alderson made the right move. La Russa, a bookworm, lawyer and animal rights advocate, is a renaissance man in the baseball fraternity. He is also a Merlin. He immediately began showing the magic that would manifest itself with three straight American League West titles beginning in 1988.

For his first bit of magic, La Russa took an overlooked pitcher named Dave Stewart and made him his ace, setting Stewart off on a spree of record-setting 20-win seasons. That was just the start of a series of moves that would affect every sector of the on-the-field product.

■ I could have used a break after leaving Chicago, but Oakland lured me with its combination of plusses. Then, the ownership (the Haas family of San Francisco, owners of Levi Strauss) was already known in baseball circles as being very fair. As for people in the front office, I had admired them when I was with the White Sox. We had wanted Carney Lansford one year (1982), and the A's front office beat us to him. They had that going for them.

The A's front office beat everyone to Jose Canseco and Mark McGwire, too. I had seen Canseco in 1985, in September. I had seen McGwire on the Olympic team twice. The White Sox had a Double-A club in Birmingham whose manager said a couple of times, "Hey, we're going to worry about the A's in a couple of years." He talked about the A's Huntsville club having lots of talent. So I looked at the Oakland farm system. They did have talent and knew how to develop it.

Then you look at the Bay Area. This is a prime major league setting. Oakland has a good ballpark, and the consistently good weather is a big plus when you're trying to win.

Having been in the same division, I'd had a good chance to look at the club. That 1986 A's club had a lot of injuries. The morale was down a little because of big expectations. The offer to manage the A's was a golden opportunity. If I'd passed on it, who knows if I'd ever get such a good shot again.

When I look back on it now, things came together very

quickly for me here. I see why: All those potential plusses that I saw when I was considering the job turned out to be actual plusses on the field and behind the scenes. From 1988 to now, there's no way we could be winning to this extent if any one of the pieces wasn't there. If the front office wasn't dynamite, we wouldn't be as good. Or if the ownership wasn't committed. They've shown the commitment. They allow you the freedom to do your job. If that wasn't there, we wouldn't have been as successful. Ditto for the farm system.

One of the healthiest things around here is that nobody tries to stand up and say, "We deserve the most credit" or "I deserve the most credit." Pitchers don't. The front office doesn't. The hitters don't. Because the truth of it is, you need everybody's piece. If you only get one or two pieces, then we're not going to win enough.

In my opinion, our attitude and the mutual respect the players have for each other are our biggest assets—and we have a lot of big assets. But the attitude on the club to be willing to come out day after day, series after series, is great. They're not trying to dominate the credit, they respect and push each other and encourage each other to give a little more. If you want to be a consistent club, which has been the hallmark of this team for three years, attitude is the key. We consistently have had great effort out there. And it's hard to do that. It's hard not to have more losses. Especially with what you face. I mean, every club's getting ready to face us. To me, with the way this club has gotten together to play time after time after time is why I say attitude is so vital.

The achievements that deserve the most credit are the ones which are built on longevity. We're starting out to make some dents on longevity. Playing good for three years, that's special. I think all of us recognize, or should recognize, that we've got that unique extra motivator or edge that can get you going sometimes. We're doing something that if we keep doing it for however long we keep it up, somebody may look back some day and say, "Boy, you know that period of Oakland A's baseball was special." The problem I see with that is, how do you get to

that point where in the year 2000 somebody will look back and say that? The only way it'll work is to take care of the immediate. You can't sit here and think about winning 95, 96 or 97 games in a season. You can't even get to, "If we can win the American League Championship Series." The only way to make it work—and it's just common sense—is to deal with the ball game you play today. Getting carried away, though, even happens to me. I'll get to some point where I'm about to go nuts with, "If this happens, then that happens, then what'll we do with the pitching rotation?" I'll start thinking about the ramifications or the consequences. And (pitching coach) Dave Duncan will say to me, "Let's win today's game." All of a sudden—instant focus. So my answer to the dynasty talk is that way out there somewhere you can be aware that we're in the midst of something special. But it's got to be way out there. Trying to win today has nothing to do with thinking about the grand scheme. The only way to make a grand scheme work is to think about today.

The difference that I've seen in the Oakland fans is that they've gotten excited. They believe in us, and they come out expecting they're going to see entertaining baseball. I feel that we've got this die-hard rabid interest in our team. The fans expect big things. I like the fans having big expectations, getting excited, but the pressure's going to be there anyway. What I'm trying to say is that I want the fans along for the ride. I think it's a great ride.

ABOVE: Shibe Park, later renamed Connie Mack Stadium in honor of the club's owner and manager, was the home of the A's thoughout their stay in Philadelphia. The Franchise began here in 1901. RIGHT: Rube Waddell led the American League with 26 wins and a 1.48 ERA in 1905, eventually making it to the Hall of Fame with a lifetime 2.16 ERA that ranks sixth all-time. PAGES 12–13: The Philadelphia Athletics of 1910–1914 were a dynasty renowned for their "$100,000 infield"—first baseman Stuffy McInnis (left), second baseman Eddie Collins (right), third baseman Frank "Home Run" Baker (center) and shortstop Jack Barry (second from right), here pictured with outfielder Danny Murphy (second from left).

FAR LEFT: Eddie Plank was one of three pitchers from the 1910–1914 A's juggernaut to wind up in the Hall of Fame. Plank had 285 of his 327 career wins for the A's. LEFT: Outfielder Napoleon "Nap" Lajoie hit .422 for the A's in 1901, which stood for 27 years as baseball's single-season mark. It still remains the A.L. record. BELOW: First baseman/third baseman Jimmie Foxx, known simply as Double-X, was the power behind the second A's dynasty of 1929–1931. He hit 100 homers those three years, reaching a career best with 58 in 1932.

ABOVE: Ty Cobb, baseball's career batting average champ, was at the end of his career when he joined the A's for two seasons in 1927–1928. A lifetime .367 hitter, Cobb hit .357 and .323 with Philadelphia before retiring at age 42.
PAGE 17, LOWER LEFT: Pitcher Chief Bender won 210 games in his career, 191 of those for the A's from 1903–1914. He also started 10 World Series games for the team, completing nine (and winning six) en route to the Hall of Fame. PAGE 17, LOWER RIGHT: Pitcher Lefty Grove (left) and catcher Mickey Cochrane (right) enjoyed unparalleled success in the A's second dynasty. Grove finished with 300 wins and Cochrane a career .320 batting average. Both made it to the Hall of Fame.

LEFT: Cornelius McGillicuddy had his name shortened to Connie Mack by newpaper editors who couldn't squeeze his name into the small columns used for box scores. He ran the A's as owner and manager for 50 years (1901–1950), a record that seems in no jeopardy now.

PAGE 18, LOWER LEFT: Roger Maris had his glory days with the New York Yankees, but he was one of a score of Yankees to first wear an A's uniform. The Kansas City teams of the late 1950s and early 1960s were often considered de facto Yankee farm teams. PAGE 18, LOWER RIGHT: The first stirrings that the A's had a new dynasty in the building stages came in 1965 in Kansas City when Bert Campaneris showed up to play shortstop. On the day this photo was taken (September 8, 1965), he played all nine positions.

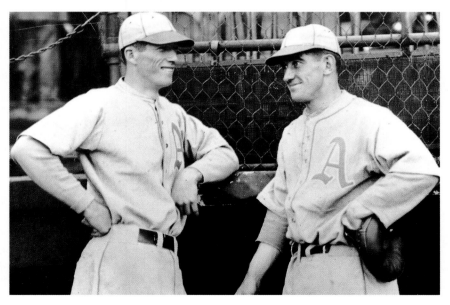

ABOVE: Following the 1954 season, the family of Connie Mack sold the A's to businessman Arnold Johnson, who made Kansas City's Municipal Stadium the club's new home. Johnson owned the team for five years before selling to Chicago insurance executive Charles O. Finley, who moved the team to Oakland for the 1968 season.
RIGHT: See captions page 17.

LEFT: One of baseball's great innovators, Charlie Finley ran the A's from 1960–1980 with a tight-fisted, hands-on philosophy that won him few friends in the A's clubhouse but which brought five straight A.L. West titles, 1971–1975, and three straight World Series championships, 1972–1974. The A's defeated the Reds in 1972, the New York Mets in 1973 (in seven games), and the Los Angeles Dodgers in 1974 (in five). Finley relaxes after the 1973 season. BELOW: Perhaps the single most vivid memory of Oakland's first World Series championship in 1972 was this catch by Joe Rudi against the Riverfront Stadium wall in Game 2. The catch, coming against the Cincinnati Reds' Denis Menke, preserved a 2-1 win for Catfish Hunter. The A's beat the Reds in seven games.

RIGHT: The A's resurgence in the early 1980s was a phenomenon known as "Billy Ball." The phrase, coined by Oakland Tribune columnist Ralph Wiley, described the hell-bent-for-leather style that those teams put forth under the direction of irascible manager Billy Martin. Martin, a Berkeley native, was a huge favorite in the Coliseum. After a strong second-place finish in 1980, Martin's A's won the American League West title in 1981. BELOW, LEFT: Third baseman Sal Bando's steady play and considerable power was at the heart of much of Oakland's success in the glory years of the 1970s. Bando was respected by his managers and team-mates alike and was the A's team captain for several years. Here he takes batting practice before the season opener in 1973. BELOW, RIGHT: Jim "Catfish" Hunter cools his arm after throwing the major league's first regular season perfect game in 46 years on May 8, 1968, in the Coliseum. Hunter won 20 games for four straight years for the A's (1971–1974) and would wind up in the Hall of Fame.

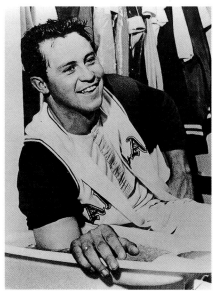

LEFT: Vida Blue took the baseball world by storm in 1971 when he went 24-8 and set an Oakland record with 301 strikeouts. Blue not only won the Cy Young Award but also was the American League's Most Valuable Player. BELOW: Reggie Jackson, whose emergence as a star took place in an Oakland uniform, came back to the A's for his final major league season in 1987 to act as the A's designated hitter and to provide veteran leadership to young sluggers like Jose Canseco and Mark McGwire. Jackson had led the A's in both home runs and RBI's in 1968, 1969, 1973, 1974 (HRs only) and 1975. This was Jackson's final at-bat in the Coliseum—against Cleveland on October 1, 1987.

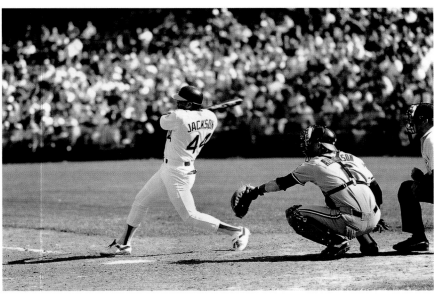

Rickey Henderson

When he was traded to New York following the 1984 season, Rickey Henderson personified everything the Oakland A's weren't.

In his last few years of his first stint with the A's, Henderson was a star on a team that didn't have another. Because of his ability to steal bases, he had name recognition throughout baseball when the team didn't. And when he was traded, he sent five able bodies to a team that didn't have enough.

Come the start of the 1989 season, Henderson still was a New York Yankee. By that time, he'd come to personify everything the A's had become. He was at the peak of his game; the defending A.L. champion A's were at the peak of their game. He was a star; Oakland had a team of stars.

The one thing the A's didn't have was an exceptional leadoff hitter. Oakland General Manager Sandy Alderson solved that with the re-acquisition of Henderson, an Oakland native who'd never lost a place in the hearts of Bay Area fans. Henderson has deep roots in the Bay Area. His childhood pal was A's starting pitcher Dave Stewart. Even when Henderson was playing for the Yankees, he bought season tickets for his mother, Bobbie.

The return of Henderson was a masterstroke. His appearance on a daily basis at the top of the lineup all but moved Oakland from the American League into a league of its own.

■ To me, as a ballplayer, my two times in Oakland have been a great way to see the ups and downs of a team. When I came here, Charlie Finley was trying to rebuild and we had really nobody. We really didn't even have fans. So to go from scraps to where we are today, it's a great sense of accomplishment. You saw progress when Roy Eisenhardt and Wally Haas picked up the club. They were interested in building a good club, promoting it and showing people that they were willing to try and bring a winner back to Oakland. They were willing to go out and sacrifice.

It's especially great for me because I grew up in Oakland,

I came out of the backyard. When I got into baseball as a kid, the A's had their dynasty club going with Reggie Jackson. You saw the excitement there, even though I felt Charlie didn't promote it like he should have. Playing here has given me a feeling of being home. It just seems like it was meant for me to be a part of all this.

If there is one game that stands out for me, it would be the first game when I came back. That feeling of waving to the fans when I first took the field, the way they cheered me on and the way that my teammates accepted me can't be topped. That day meant more to me than anything. Because when I was flying back here right after the trade, I'd been wondering what was going to happen and how

were they going to react to me. I think they were very special to me. They all accepted me. During my time with New York, when I'd come back to Oakland, I'd always heard a lot of cheers. They were all waiting for that moment when Rickey Henderson came back. I always heard people yelling, "Rickey, when are you going to come back?" I'd always say I'd be back, because they wanted it so much. But I didn't know what was going to happen. It just so happened that it did happen.

A lot of time you can go to a new club and see some of the great players in the game. What made coming to Oakland so special to me is that the players respected one another. They pulled for one another. They gave everybody the same credit, no matter who you were. That's what really turns me on more than anything. Rookie or veteran, they respect you as a player.

I don't carry the club. I see myself as a guy who carries a part of the club. No one does it alone. Togetherness is one of the best things about this club. I think I can give the club a spark. I think sometimes the guys pick up what I do and it brings the best out of them. And I get the same lift from watching Carney Lansford or Jose Canseco or Dave Henderson.

I have to bury the desire to steal bases sometimes, because a lot of the time this club doesn't need the steals. We have a club with great hitters and a lot of power, and you don't need to go out and run crazy. My first time in Oakland, we didn't have that. So I had to go out and steal bases to make things happen. Now anybody on this team can make things happen.

There are a lot of us who are homegrown, and that adds a lot of flavor to the club. We know what home is about and just how much winning means to the fans. As a kid when you go to the playground and you have your mother and your father there, and they watch you play, they see you win, and they're so excited. So now, we're playing in front of fans all over the world, but we're still playing for our families and in front of them. It makes us want to succeed all the more.

I had a great baseball experience in New York. I think the players I played with taught me a lot about being an

outstanding ball player or shooting for goals you want to achieve and loving the game enough to go out and play hard.

I appreciate the game more now that I'm older and more experienced. I'm having a lot of fun now. I'm having fun because I appreciate the game more. I love the game more. I want to do something special. I want to teach the younger generation about the game just like others have taught me. A lot of people look at this game as a business. They say if you're having too much fun, you're not into the game. I say, fun *is* the game. That is why we're out here. Sure, we're serious about winning ball games and about what our jobs require. Still, if you don't get joy out of what you're doing, then it's not right.

To tell you the truth, I'd like to keep at baseball for as long as Pete Rose did or anybody else did. I don't see the end right now. Not at all. I want to play as long as I can.

A's Present

ABOVE: The Rites of Spring, Phoenix, March 1990. A's limber up in the early Arizona morning preparing for the long grind of the season. PAGE 27, TOP: April 9, 1990, Oakland Coliseum. Mack Newton helps Mike Gallego stretch on opening night. PAGE 27, BOTTOM: March 1990. Carney Lansford and Rickey Henderson work out in the weight room in Phoenix, Arizona. PAGES 24–25: May 4, 1990. Dave Stewart fires a fastball past Dwight Evans on his way to winning another duel over Boston's Roger Clemens at the Coliseum.

RIGHT: April 1989, Oakland Coliseum. Tony La Russa jots down one of his frequent notes, here during a game against Detroit. BELOW: May 21, 1989, Oakland. Rene Lachemann, A's third-base coach, reviews A's victory over Boston. After each game he logs the location of every pitch thrown.
PAGE 29, TOP: May 26, 1990, Oakland Coliseum. Rickey Henderson, on his way to stealing third base, tying the all-time American League base-stealing record, against the Cleveland Indians.
PAGE 29, BOTTOM: Spring training, 1990. Oakland A's ride the bus to Mesa, Arizona, for a "Cactus League" encounter with the Chicago Cubs.

LEFT: April 22, 1990, Oakland Coliseum. Rickey Henderson rounds third and heads for home in A's come-from-behind win over Seattle. BELOW: May 30, 1990, Oakland Coliseum. A's pitching coach Dave Duncan meets with his catchers in the clubhouse before each game. Here he goes over pitching strategies against the Toronto line-up. Left to right: Jamie Quirk, Duncan, Ron Hassey, and Terry Steinbach. PAGE 30: April 30, 1989, Oakland Coliseum. Mike Gallego turns a double play in A's–Detroit game.

Dave Stewart

Of all the paths that led great performers to Oakland, none was tougher to travel than Dave Stewart's.

An up-and-coming star for the Los Angeles Dodgers, he found himself traded to Texas, where success and Stewart were distant relatives at best. He went one entire season, 1985, without winning a game. After a brief spin with Philadelphia in late 1985 and early 1986, the Phillies released him.

The A's, struggling for pitching at the time, took a chance on the local kid from St. Elizabeth's High. Later that season, the A's hired Tony La Russa. He took a chance on Stewart, too, picking him to start in his Oakland managerial debut. Stewart beat Roger Clemens and Boston on national television. Just like that, a star was born.

From that time on, he's been baseball's winningest pitcher, including four straight 20-win seasons. More than that, he's thrown himself into the community in which he was raised and was subsequently recognized for his anti-drug and youth activities. At the 1990 All-Star game he was named winner of baseball's Roberto Clemente award for community involvement.

■ Playing at home is a very good situation for me. I couldn't ask for much better than to be pitching at home and to be pitching well at home. You'd be surprised what effect being around your family and friends has. I think that's been the biggest part of my determination to succeed. I'm more determined because I don't want to be embarrassed at home. That's been a great part for me in winning here and in being successful the last couple of years.

There's a lot of recognition. As a matter of fact, I can't go any place in the area and not be recognized. I can't go bicycling or be sitting around shooting the breeze with friends. Notoriety in the area is much greater now than it's ever been. I think my involvement in the community has a lot to do with it because when I do talk to people, they tend to say, "Stew, you're a great pitcher but your community involvement is just outstanding—it means so much to the kids and to us as adults." So I know that has a great deal to do with it. Sometimes when I feel like grabbing a bite to eat or seeing a movie, the notoriety is hard. It's amazing how people think you can sign autographs in the dark at the movies. You want to relax, have a plain and simple quiet time. Sometimes you need that. It's tough to separate, though, because people in general get me going. If a person comes up and is generally enthusiastic about the game or, for that matter, what I'm doing in my career, it's easy to get into the conversation.

Being on a championship club in Oakland has meant a lot to me. I read in the newspapers from time to time that a lot of people feel that the club and its motion forward is attributed some to me, to my success, to my being able to

maybe be a leader for a pitching staff and be a leader for our team. And to have somebody say that, I'm very flattered. I feel honored to be associated on that level with that team. Again, it becomes a pride thing.

It's been hard work, but nothing beats the day-to-day challenge of watching us play and seeing if I can help us win when my day comes around. That's the fun part of it. And when it's all over and done with, you look back on the season and say, "What did we accomplish?" We have done good things here and have some really remarkable accomplishments. And I don't think we're finished yet.

It's great when you can have a good time and when the team's winning. We have fun in the clubhouse, we have fun away from the clubhouse and we have fun during the game. We're not best buddies, but we're buddies. Each and every player in this clubhouse is a friend to each other. Most clubs that I've played on have been clique-ish. One group will go its way, then five or six other guys will go another way, and five or six more will go another way. You don't find the mixing and matching in most places that you do in this clubhouse, and that makes things work here.

Tony (La Russa) has been the best manager I've ever played for in terms of communication. I don't have to guess where he's coming from. I know where he's coming from. I know a lot of times when I'm pitching a ball game, I have a real good idea of what he's thinking. That comes from the way he communicates with a guy. That means talking to him not just during the season but talking in the off-season, too. I can't say more than say he's the best manager I've ever played for and this is the best player-manager relationship I've ever had. That's one reason this is the best baseball's ever been for me.

One of the things that is most gratifying to the players is the fan support. Most clubs have great nighttime attendance and weekend attendance. Most parks do their business on the weekend. But we draw during the week. Day games, night games, every day of the week we have 25,000 or 30,000. The fans have matured that way. They've also matured in the sense that they have a pretty good idea what the game is about, how it's played. They've got a pretty good idea of our style as a team. It helps when the club is winning. When the club is winning, the fans follow you closer on TV and in the papers. When you don't have a winning tradition, you don't hold interest. We're starting to get the tradition of winning.

Oakland has always had a tradition of winners with the Raiders and the early A's. We lost it with the baseball part. So what we're trying to do is regain what we've lost. I think we're on the verge of doing that. We've made moves in that direction, but we want to be winning for a long time. We've got players who are going to be around a long time who have the ability to carry on the tradition. These guys have the knowledge of what it takes to win again and again.

LEFT: June 9, 1990, Oakland Coliseum. Felix Jose races in for a shoe-top catch in A's–Kansas City duel. BELOW: May 13, 1990, Oakland Coliseum. Rickey Henderson steals second as Cal Ripkin, Jr., waits for the throw in A's battle with Baltimore. PAGE 34: April 16, 1988, Oakland Coliseum. Dennis Eckersley (without shirt) and Gene Nelson discuss the finer points of pitching in the Oakland clubhouse before the game.

Oakland power at the plate.
LEFT: Mark McGwire in first game of
ALCS, October 3, 1989. CENTER: Rickey
Henderson in the SkyDome, October 6,
1989. RIGHT: Dave Parker in Game 4 of
the 1989 World Series in Candlestick
Park. PAGE 37, TOP: Dave Henderson
in Game 4 of the 1989 World Series.
PAGE 37, BOTTOM: Jose Canseco at
the Coliseum, May 27, 1990.

Carney Lansford

No one has a better perspective on the lows and highs of the Oakland experience in the 1980s than Carney Lansford.

The one-time batting champ (1981, with Boston) came to the A's after the 1982 season and in the middle 1980s suffered through personal and professional crises. He and his wife, Debbie, lost their son Nicholas to kidney disease in the first few weeks of their first year in Oakland. By his fourth year, Lansford almost couldn't wait to leave what he perceived as a floundering organization.

All that has changed in the last few seasons, however, with the on-field rebirth of the A's. The San Jose–born-and-raised third baseman has been instrumental in helping with the delivery. He nearly won the 1989 A.L. batting title, losing on the final day of the season to Minnesota's Kirby Puckett.

One of the best students of the game in the A's club-house, Lansford is the team's player representative and de facto captain.

■ The last several years, since the middle of 1986, have been outstanding. The front office has gone out and made a total commitment to win. They've gone out and gotten the talent it takes to win—and at a high price. But if you're going to win, that's the thing you're going to have to do. You've got to pay the price.

Before that, forget it. The first three years I was with the A's, I'd just kind of like to forget those times. We didn't have a lot of talent on those teams. And to be frank, we didn't have good managers. That was very difficult. Especially when you've played for a good manager. I knew as a player that there were moves being made which were not right. But you have to bite your tongue, because it's not your decision. Of course, that all changed when we brought Tony (La Russa) over.

To be honest, when the 1986 season started, I didn't even want to come back to the A's. I didn't have any desire. I knew we weren't going anywhere. With Tony, it was like being born again. Things started going right. Decisions started being made right. When you are around

it long enough and enough things go wrong for a long period of time, you start wondering whether it's you or the club that's bad. Are you the one who's messed up?

But when you bring somebody like Tony over and he starts making the right moves and he commands the respect that he does, then I knew it hadn't been me. It became fun again. Baseball in Oakland has been a roller-coaster, but it's been a smooth ride for the last three and a half years, even though we've had the number of injuries we've had.

When you play for a guy who has one desire, and that is to win, you're a better player. And Tony told us up front that if we didn't play like we were capable of playing or if

we don't give 100 percent to this team, we wouldn't be around. That's the bottom line —he doesn't accept anything less. And to this day, that hasn't changed.

It's great to be in Oakland, because everybody on this club gets along. Tony wanted to get a certain type of person here. He weeded out the people he didn't think would fit into his plans as the type of players he liked. The organization is very conscious about getting a certain type of player around here because they don't want to ruin a good thing. We really do have good clubhouse chemistry, and guys get along well. I've been on teams where they don't get together very often off the field, but that's not true with this team. We get together.

Sometimes I think the (Oakland) fans have almost gotten complacent. It's almost like they've come to expect us to win. And when we don't, it's like, "What's going on with the A's? How come they're not winning?" What they don't realize is that throughout the course of the last few seasons, we've won despite battling through injuries year after year. This has been no cakewalk for us, we're battling our tails off. We're scratching and clawing trying to win. We're banged up come August and September every year. Guys can't get a day off to stay strong like they should. If fans understood that, that would be good. What they think is that after what we've done the last few years and with the talent we have here, we're supposed to automatically win. Well, it doesn't work that way. We still need the fans' support. They need to understand, it's been a rough road for us.

It's been nice, though, that most of the fans seem to realize that. The front office has put some outstanding talent on the field and made the park an enjoyable place for people to want to come and want to watch games. And that I think is the nicest part of the whole thing in Oakland for the fans of the A's, seeing the yearly attendance increases. I was born and raised in the Bay Area. I remember coming here in the early 1970s when Charlie Finley (the Oakland A's owner through August 1980) was here with back-to-back-to-back World Series. I remember coming to Opening Night the next year. You could have any seat in the house. To me, as a kid in high school, that was unbelievable. I couldn't understand the people around here. You shouldn't be able to get a ticket to watch three-time world champions. The Haases (who bought the team from Finley) have done something really special. You've

got to give them a lot of credit.

They improved the stadium. They've improved the talent. It's a fun place to come. The players here, you never know what to expect from them. You never know what you're going to get when you come to an A's game. You don't know who's going shine that day, because anybody can.

We have the opportunity to be one of the great teams. That's the nice thing. It seems like every year it's never easy. Then they go out and get Willie McGee and Harold Baines. How can you not want to go out and play hard and win for an organization like that? You try extra hard for a club like that.

It sure has been much nicer. There have been a few bumps, but we know where we're coming from, what we're trying to achieve, and the champagne the last couple of years is what it's all about. We've almost come to expect that at the end of the year. It would be almost a funny feeling not to pop the champagne at the end of the season with the A's. We have the confidence, we have the talent, but I think we have the makeup—more than anything else, that helps.

ABOVE AND BELOW: May 30, 1990, Oakland Coliseum. Jose Canseco engages in clubhouse hijinks, while Rickey Henderson and Dave Stewart contemplate domino dominance, before the A's meet the Toronto Blue Jays.

LEFT: June 12, 1990, Oakland Coliseum. Willie Randolph takes throw from catcher as a Texas Ranger steals second. BELOW: April 4, 1990, Candlestick Park, San Francisco. Gene Nelson wheels and deals in the preseason Bay Bridge series clash.

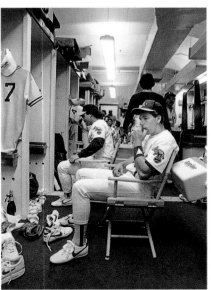

ABOVE: October 15, 1988, Dodger Stadium. Dennis Eckersley and Dave Henderson talk before the first game of the World Series. Next to Eckersley, from right to left, are teammates Eric Plunk, Todd Burns, and Matt Sinatro, and coaches Mike Paul, Dave McKay, and Jim "Frenchie" Lefebvre. LEFT: October 20, 1988, Oakland Coliseum. Walt Weiss stares dejectedly into the future, moments after A's lose the fifth game and the World Series to the Dodgers. PAGE 42, TOP: October 14, 1989, Oakland Coliseum. Dave "Parkway" Parker receives home-run greeting after putting A's ahead of Giants in the first game of the World Series. PAGE 42, BOTTOM: July 15, 1990, Oakland Coliseum. Lead-off hitter Rickey Henderson watches a fastball all the way into B. J. Surhoff's glove in A's–Milwaukee game.

THIS PAGE: May 12, 1990, Oakland Coliseum. Dave Henderson races in to snatch a sinking liner and quash an Oriole rally. PAGE 44: June 1989, Oakland Coliseum. Tony La Russa gives umpires the what-for.

Bob Welch

Bob Welch can't circumvent the laws of physics. Those laws say that there can never be any such thing as a perpetual motion machine. So Welch isn't one.

But he's close. Of all of the Oakland A's, Welch is the foremost mover and shaker. He's not one to sit still, not when there's a chance to be active, to be involved.

It was like that in Los Angeles, too, for the Detroit-born right-hander. He found success in a Dodger uniform. But it was with Oakland, following a trade in the winter after the 1987 season, that Welch found stardom, culminating in his becoming baseball's winningest pitcher in 1990.

It has been a star-crossed time for Welch. The only member of the A's to live in San Francisco, Welch and his wife, Mary Ellen, were uprooted when the home they had just finished building in the Marina District was severely damaged by the October 17, 1989, earthquake, the same 7.1 monster that delayed the Oakland–San Francisco World Series for 10 days. The damage was so extensive that they weren't able to move in until after the 1990 season was underway.

A few months earlier, their first son, Dillon, had been born. A day later, Welch's mother died. Bob and Mary Ellen Welch became parents again in September 1990 of another boy, Riley. On the 21st of that month Welch became baseball's first 25-game winner in a decade.

But back in 1988, when Welch first changed out of Dodger Blue and into Oakland green and gold, he had no presentiment that he was going to get more than just a new wardrobe.

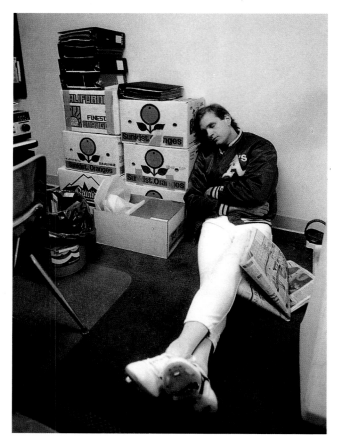

■ I had a lot of success with Tommy Lasorda doing the managing in Los Angeles while I was there. But Tony La Russa has been different for me, and he's really helped. Through (pitching coach) Dave Duncan, he has us undertake a different type of preparation for the game, and he's done one hell of a job. If there's something that will help me, he's going to say it. And if there's something I feel I need to do or say, I'm going to share it with him. Before, with Tommy Lasorda, we had some great baseball seasons in Los Angeles. But I think Tony's as prepared as anybody I've ever seen, and he gets his team that way, too.

There's no doubt that preparation has made the difference for me here in Oakland. If I don't get ready to pitch against the Seattle Mariners or Detroit Tigers four days before it happens, then when the day comes, I can't just walk out there and walk away a winner. I've worked more on the mental approach to the game under Dunc and Tony, and I think you see the results on the field. Baseball doesn't work as well when the focus isn't quite there.

If I go out to the mound and have everything, if all my pitches are working and I've got great stuff, well, hell, anybody can pitch like that. People look at a guy who's hot and say, "Geez, he looks unbeatable." Well, sure. Who

doesn't look unbeatable when everything is going his way? But it's the time that you feel a little sore or a little tired or a little run down, that's when all the preparation really pays off, when you're struggling mentally or physically. When you're on, you don't need anybody's advice.

There are times when you wake up in the morning and you can't wait to pitch, that you know you're going to throw great. And then there are times when you wake up and you feel, "Hey, my back's sore" or "I'm beat up from travel" or whatever. When that happens, you start playing mind games with yourself. If you haven't made the right preparations a couple of days in advance, you won't be ready. And you'll probably get rocked. That's the main thing that Tony brings to this club. There's never a day when we aren't ready to go out and win.

There's no doubt about it that our attitude is what makes this team different. It's very powerful. You sit and talk to guys here and you learn very quickly that baseball basically is pretty simple—you play the game hard today and, hell, you worry about the next one when it comes along. With our talent and our ability, if we do that consistently during the course of the season we're going to win a lot of baseball games. That's what Tony preaches, and that's the way it's happened.

You can see what's happened the last three Septembers. It's a long, grueling season. It gets tiring, sure, but if people have a good attitude, a good chemistry and a good team, it'll pay off, especially when you have the ability that this team has. We take pride in playing well down the stretch. And when we've needed a boost, the front office has given us a big uplift. When you see a Willie McGee or a Harold Baines come over, it gives the guys a big charge. Then you get to the point of the season where you start smelling it, and you're ready to charge.

I had never won 20 games in a season, much less 25, so to be in a position to win those games this year was special to me. But the one game I think I'll remember the most was not either of those. It was my first game of the 1990 season. I'd pitched in three games during spring training. I had a 17.72 ERA, and I'd pitched awful. There's no other word for it. But the thing about baseball is, to have some success, sometimes you've got to take your lumps first. I took my lumps in the spring, but when the season started, that first game (against Seattle, a 5–3 Welch win) I seemed to get over the hump. Getting off on the right foot after that spring was so important. The 10-game winning streak and everything else that happened, I think, goes right back to that first win over Seattle.

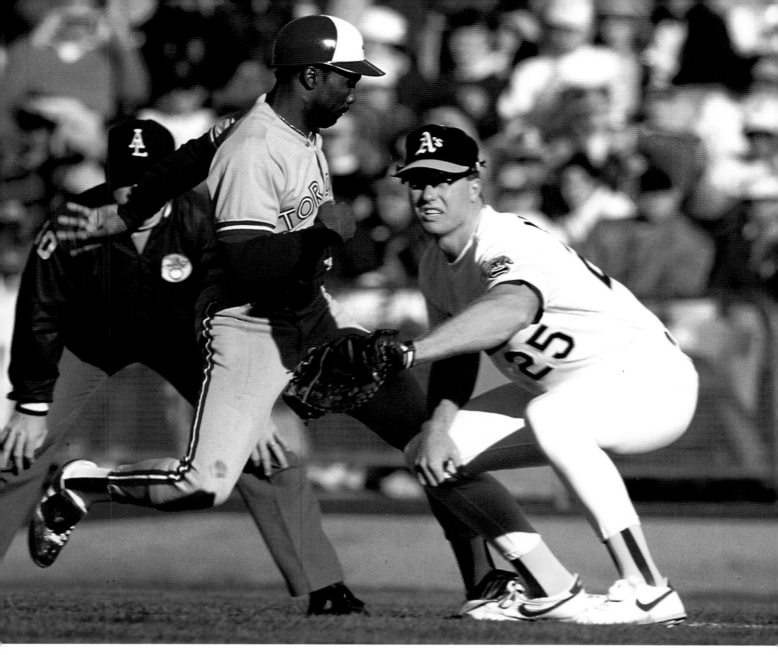

ABOVE: May 28, 1990, Oakland Coliseum. Mookie Wilson dances back to first base as Mark McGwire takes the throw from the mound in A's–Toronto contest.
RIGHT: August 12, 1990, Oakland Coliseum. Willie Randolph turns the double play against his old teammates from New York.

RIGHT: October 1988, Fenway Park, Boston. From left to right: Dave Parker, Wally Haas, Bob Welch, Dave Stewart and Jose Canseco (sitting) watch the replay of Jose's home run in the second game of the ALCS in Boston.
BELOW: August 30, 1990, Oakland Coliseum. Harold Baines talks to the press before taking the field against Kansas City in his first game in an Oakland uniform.

THIS PAGE, LEFT: May 1988, Oakland Coliseum. Jose Canseco can't quite get to a drive down the right-field line. BELOW: May 1988, Oakland Coliseum. Left to right: Detroit manager Sparky Anderson, 49er head coach Bill Walsh, and Tony La Russa swap tall tales before the Tigers meet the Athletics. PAGE 50: August 11, 1989, Anaheim Stadium. Dave Henderson streaks around second on his way to a triple in A's important win over the Angels.

Mark McGwire

Mark McGwire was hardly an unknown when he was drafted by the A's in the summer of 1984. He'd been a star for the University of Southern California, the prototypical collegiate baseball power. He was a star on the first United States Olympic baseball team, where he was such a force that another All-American first baseman, Mississippi State's Will Clark, had to move to left field so as to accommodate both booming bats.

But nothing—not his All-American status or his Olympic silver medal—prepared the baseball world for Mark McGwire's major league debut.

Winning the first base job two weeks into the 1987 season, McGwire went on an unrelenting home-run tear, hitting 49 while driving in 118 runs as the second of three straight Oakland players to be named American League Rookie of the Year.

Since then, he's gone on to become the first man in baseball history with 30 or more home runs in his first four seasons and has averaged over 100 RBIs per season as well.

For early-arriving fans at many A's day home games, McGwire frequently can be seen not at first base but in the outfield, playing catch with his son, Matthew, on whom he dotes.

Four seasons of success in Oakland have produced a subtle change in the outlook on life of the Orange County–born-and-raised McGwire, who was a confirmed advocate of the Southern California lifestyle when he broke in with the A's.

■ All this has made me a lover of Northern California. I grew up thinking I'd never, ever live out of Southern California for my entire life. Then all of a sudden, I'm building a house up here and I'm planning on living here no matter what happens to me in baseball.

As far as baseball, I don't think you can ask for anything else after what we've done in the time I've been here. When I got drafted in 1984, I really didn't know what was going to happen to me.

I first got called up to the big leagues less than two years after I signed out of USC. Then to do what I did in 1987 and to go to the World Series in my second year of major league baseball and to win a World Series in my third year, it's been a unique experience.

When I look back on 1987, in some ways I still can't believe what happened. I went from a guy who barely made the team to magazine covers. Players who had played for 15 years had never had to put up with what I did as a rookie. I never wanted to be in the public eye. I had never been one to say no to demands on my time, but things became ridiculous. But you grow and mature, and I learned from the experience what I can give to the media and the

fans and what I can't. The best thing I can give them is to go out every day, or nearly every day, and play hard. If I do that, the numbers will follow. I've always believed that, and when you look at what this team has done the last few years, I think we all believe that.

In some ways, I think people must think I've played in the majors for 10 or 12 years, because I've been lucky to experience so much. But it's really been such a short time. An amazingly short time. I've only played for four seasons now. It's just that so much great stuff has been crammed into a short time. Rookie of the Year. The World Series. The championship in 1989. Sometimes it becomes hard to believe it's all happened so quickly.

I guess if you want to say I've had the luck of the draw in being in Oakland while all these great things have happened, I'd have to agree. What I really want to do is to thank all the people who passed me up in the 1984 draft. I was taken by Oakland as the 10th pick, so nine teams had to pass on me.

One of the reasons I've had a great four years is that the organization has made just such a big effort to become a winner. And that's what it takes. And a lot of organizations I don't think will do that. To Sandy Alderson and the Haases, winning is a big thing. They showed it back in 1988 when they went and got all those free agents and put them together with the nucleus of the youngsters who grew up in the minor league system. It's worked out. They just showed again how serious they are by going out and doing what we did this year, getting Harold Baines and Willie McGee.

To my way of thinking, all this winning started deep in the organization. A lot of us grew up through the minor league organization, and a lot of us had winning attitudes down there because we learned how to win down there—and we did win as minor leaguers. Now it's rubbed off up here.

Playing for Tony La Russa. That helps, too. A lot of people might say with another manager we'd be doing the same things we've done the last few years. I don't think so. It takes a special kind of manager to put a team out on the field. We have a lot of talent here, but you can have all the talent in the world and not necessarily win.

Tony makes it easier for us to go out and play by the things he does. You almost never see him make a mistake. He's so on top of the game, he makes our lives here so much easier.

I just don't know how baseball could be much better. I'm very happy here. As far as I'm concerned. I wouldn't care to play for another ball club. You can't ever tell what's going to happen in baseball, but we have a chance to be something special for a long time, and I want to be part of it. I think every player in the clubhouse wants to be part of it.

The fans here are great. For three years in a row they've broken attendance records. The crowds are just getting bigger and bigger. We've got great weather. We'll play other clubs and they'll be talking about playing an entire homestand on blazing hot Astroturf at 140 degrees. They come here and look how comfortable it is to play, and they're envious. So that has a lot to do with being happy. When you're on the road and playing in a lot of hot and humid cities, you know you're going to come home and be comfortable. That might add a few years on to your career, too.

These four years have been a unique ride. I've enjoyed every minute of it. I mean, there have been a lot of ups and downs, but the bottom line is we're winning and everybody's having some fun. It's been a great ride so far. Winning's contagious, right? When you get that winning feeling and taste, you don't ever want to give it up. I think that's what's going through this organization. We don't want to give up the feeling as long as we have a chance to win. I think the fans see it, too.

A couple of years down the line, depending on how this team goes and does, we'll probably sit back and say, "Wow, remember what we did?" It's really unbelievable.

ABOVE: May 1988, Oakland Coliseum. Oakland's Tony Phillips and Boston's Sam Horn and Ellis Burks work out in the communal weight room after A's game with the Red Sox. RIGHT: July 10, 1990, Oakland Coliseum. A's phenom Todd van Poppel on the day of his signing, with Athletics director of baseball information Jay Alves pointing to the future.

LEFT AND BELOW: April 22, 1990,
Oakland Coliseum. Walt Weiss takes
the throw and applies the tag to a
sliding Ken Griffey, Jr., in A's contest
with Seattle.

THIS PAGE, RIGHT: May 30, 1990, Oakland Coliseum. Walt Weiss dives into third as Toronto's Kelly Gruber waits for the throw. BELOW: July 25, 1990, Oakland Coliseum. Todd Burns comes in from the bull pen in A's battle with the Angels. PAGE 57: July 10, 1990, Wrigley Field, Chicago. The two all-time stolen-base leaders, Rickey Henderson and Lou Brock, chat before the All-Star game in Chicago.

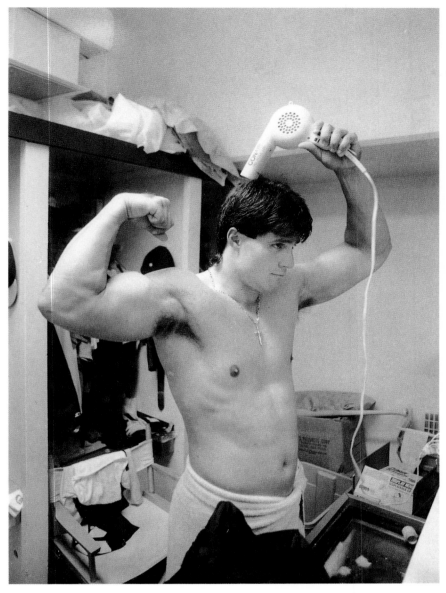

THIS PAGE, LEFT: June 1990, Oakland Coliseum. After the game, Jose Canseco works out with blow dryer in front of the mirror. THIS PAGE, BELOW: August 8, 1990, Oakland Coliseum. Scott Sanderson is on the hill as the A's take on Baltimore. PAGE 58, TOP: July 26, 1990, Oakland Coliseum. Jamie Quirk reaches for a throw as Brian Downing dives across the plate in A's game with California. PAGE 58, BOTTOM LEFT: May 1989, Oakland Coliseum grounds keeper Mark Razum, an artist with dirt and grass, massages the home-plate area. PAGE 58, BOTTOM RIGHT: June 1989, Oakland Coliseum. Oakland equipment manager, Frank Ciensczyk, and his assistant, Jimmy Sasaki, check A's luggage on get-away day.

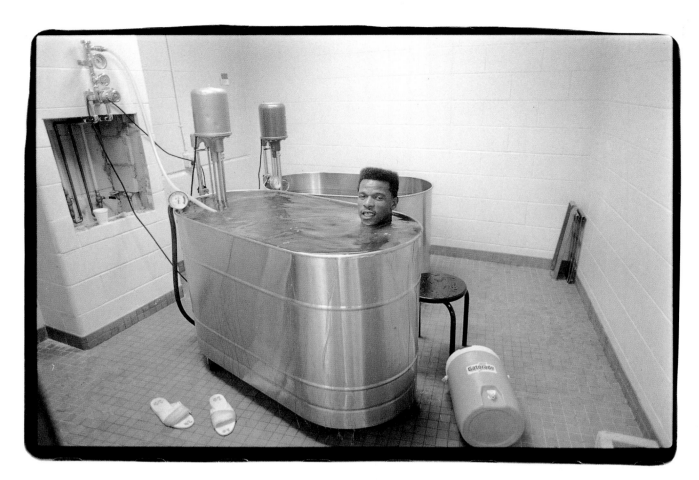

ABOVE: October 1989, SkyDome, Toronto. Rickey Henderson bobs in the whirlpool before taking the field to lead the A's to victory in the fifth game of the American League Championship Series. THIS PAGE, RIGHT: May 1990, Oakland Coliseum. A's trainer Barry Weinberg wraps the arm of the Eckman after Dennis earns another save. PAGE 61: October 7, 1989, SkyDome, Toronto. An exultant Dennis Eckersley raises his hands in victory as the A's beat Toronto to win the ALCS.

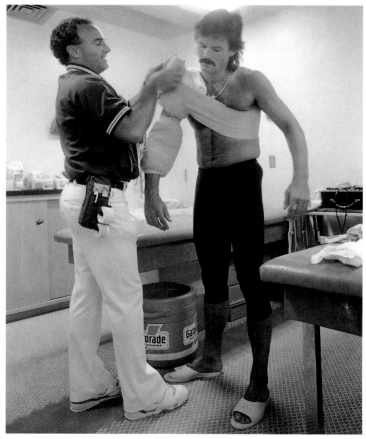

Dave Henderson

Dave Henderson showed up on Oakland's doorstep all but unwanted after the San Francisco Giants opted not to re-sign him following the 1987 season. Henderson was coming off a bad year, and to some people it didn't look like much of a move when the A's signed the center fielder as a free agent.

Some people were wrong. Major league wrong. Henderson, from the San Joaquin Valley town of Dos Palos, came into his stride from Game 1 of the 1988 season. He homered in that first game and never let up en route to establishing himself not only as the A's everyday center fielder, but as the A.L.'s Comeback Player of the Year as well.

Henderson, whose trademark is his gap-toothed grin, is one of the most popular of the A's among his teammates. They respect his biting wit in the clubhouse—his specialty is good-natured but stinging verbal abuse in quantities measured to keep the clubhouse loose—in addition to his slashing bat and deft glove on the field.

He has proven to be among the most durable of the A's as well, playing on demand until arthroscopic surgery on his knee derailed him for a month near the end of the 1990 season.

Off the field his contributions to the community were recognized when he was given the A's 1990 Walter A. Haas, Jr., Community Achievement Award.

■ I think we sort of surprised people in 1988. We won 100-something games. Before that, everybody thought we were good, but they didn't know how good. The last two years they knew how good we were, and we still went out and won. Everybody knows it's tougher to win when people know you're supposed to win, but even so, I'm not at all surprised at the success of the 1989 and 1990 teams.

I think we have an edge because man-per-man we have so many ways to beat you. Against every team we play, we can do two of the three parts of the game (pitching, defense and offense) real well and beat you. The big difference between us and the other guys is that we don't have to do everything right to beat you. We've won games where we've made two or three errors or didn't pitch real well and won anyway. And when we go out on the field, we have that "we know we're going to win" kind of attitude. If a couple guys have a good day, we know we're going to win.

How you accept losing depends on how you lose. If somebody beats you, you have to recognize the difference between that and going out and losing the ball game yourself. Because sometimes you get beat, and there's nothing you can do about it. But if you sit around and give away three games and get swept, that can make this team angry. Making us angry tends to make us play real good baseball and win five, six, seven in a row. I don't think we get too excited if we get beat. Or discouraged or panicky.

About the only thing that can rattle this team is a fastball at the neck. We've got a few guys who get pissed off at a fastball at the neck. Other than that, there's no reason to be rattled ever, given the attitude of this team, knowing that we're consistently going to play solid baseball.

I think for a manager to be successful, he has to have good timing, especially when he says certain things. All managers get angry and yell and scream and throw things. But you have to have good timing with those things. More than anything, Tony La Russa really has that kind of timing. He not only knows what to say but when to say it. And when to say nothing.

You've got to put the right guys on the field, too. The bottom line is, you've got to have the horses, and we've got horses here. The other teams I've played for, they didn't quite have enough horses, and the manager didn't have any choice but to lose the pennant or to lose the playoffs.

Another thing about Tony is that he expects to win not only with the front-line guys, but with everyone. I don't think he ever puts anybody into a game not expecting to win. You wouldn't be on this team if you couldn't help.

I've had a lot of fun in baseball, even in losing 104 games. That has gotten me into trouble, but that's the way it goes. I think I'll have fun no matter what, so to say this is the most fun I've ever had is a tough call for me. But to cap it off with a world championship—that's not fun as much as it is achieving a goal. Fun is just having a job and being able to play every day and show what you can do. But coming out of spring training and going on to win the whole thing, that's achieving a goal. You need a different adjective for that—maybe respect.

This team is looking for respect, and 10 years down the road people are going to remember these years like they do the 1972–1974 Oakland teams. It's important for us to put our names in there with the dynasty-type teams. When you start winning three championships in a row, you become well known and you break a lot of records, you do a lot of things right, so you're going to be remembered if you do it day-in, day-out, year-in, year-out. So that's important for us. By the time we're done, they might make one of those highlight films like they made about the 49ers or something.

No matter how it looks to anyone on the outside, none of this has come easy. When we look back, 1988 was easy, but only compared to 1989 or 1990. But I don't think anything comes easy. Like the old saying, you just don't

throw your gloves, bats and balls out there to bring home a world championship. You've got to go through the bumps and bruises and the operations and all that stuff. You've got to put out to appreciate it. Believe me, we appreciate this success.

A lot of people point to me in the post-season and say that I rise to the occasion, but actually that's wrong. I think I see a change in other people. I'm the same nut. I think other people are so tense and World Series–minded that I'm the only relaxed guy on the field. That's why I do well. You can't play good with one hand around your throat. That's why they make me look good. Over the years I have seen pitchers are not quite the same in World Series play. Consequently they get raked, and usually by me.

One of the things that makes this club special is the way that we've rallied together, being willing to play hurt when other guys were on the disabled list. And it didn't just happen for one game or one week, but for a lot of times in the last few years. That will stick with us a long time, longer than winning the World Series championship rings, even. That's the stuff we get to remember. The fans and the media get to remember all the stats, the home runs and all that junk. We remember picking a guy up when he's down, helping a guy out when he's injured. Stuff like that. That's the inside family.

THIS PAGE, LEFT: October 6, 1990, SkyDome, Toronto. Tony La Russa relieves Bob Welch as Ron Hassey looks on in A's eventual 6-5 win over the Blue Jays in ALCS Game 4. THIS PAGE, BELOW: May 1990, Oakland Coliseum. A's bull pen lounges in the sun. PAGE 64, TOP: July 10, 1990, Wrigley Field, Chicago. Mark McGwire looks on with the Royals' Bret Saberhagen as (seated, left to right) Ken Griffey, Jr., George Bell, the Rocket (Roger Clemens), and Rickey Henderson play cards during the rain delay in the All-Star game. PAGE 64, BOTTOM: June 1989, Oakland Coliseum. Dave Henderson dresses at his locker prior to batting practice.

THIS PAGE, RIGHT: July 22, 1990, Oakland Coliseum. Rickey Henderson goes back to the wall to rob Kelly Gruber of extra bases in A's–Blue Jay contest. BELOW, LEFT: October 3, 1989, Oakland Coliseum. Terry Steinbach goes back to the screen to grab a foul pop-up in first game of the American League Championship Series with Toronto. BELOW, RIGHT: March 1990, Mesa, Arizona. Carney Lansford, shoulder wrapped in ice, chats with trainer Larry Davis in late inning of A's spring training game with the Cubs. PAGE 67: October 10, 1990, Oakland Coliseum. Sandy Alderson, Rickey Henderson, and Rene Lachemann douse each other in postgame merriment after the A's sweep the BoSox.

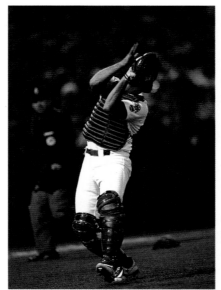

PROFILE   Jose Canseco

From the first, Jose Canseco turned tremendous potential into headline-grabbing numbers.

Baltimore pitcher Mike Flanagan nicknamed him Jose No-Mistake-O after seeing him launch a couple of bombs en route to 33 homers and 117 RBIs and the 1986 Rookie of the Year award. In an early-season game in Anaheim, California Angels designated hitter Reggie Jackson was awestruck. "He hits them where I hit them. That's scary," the left-handed Jackson said after the right-handed Canseco crushed an opposite-field homer.

Two years later, Canseco was acclaimed as the best in baseball. He became the first player in history to hit 40 homers and steal 40 bases in a season. "Mr. 40-40" led the A's to their first World Series appearance in 15 years with a .307 batting average, 42 homers and a club record 124

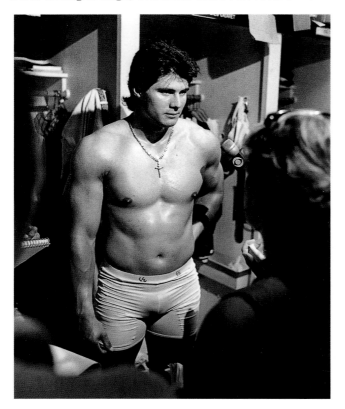

RBIs. Along the way he picked up the American League's Most Valuable Player award.

The Havana-born slugger then had two star-crossed years. He missed the first half of the 1989 season after breaking a bone in his left wrist, but returned with a big second half and postseason that helped the A's defeat the Giants in the World Series. And in 1990, he was en route to another monster season until a recurring back problem in August and a finger injury in September hampered his hitting.

Canseco's ascension to MVP and beyond has made him the most recognizable face in an Oakland clubhouse full of recognizable faces.

■ The speed of our success from 1985 when I came up to now has to come as something of a surprise to me. I came up when the rosters were expanded in 1985, in September. To me, even though I was just a kid at the time, it seemed that the team was a shambles. The way the players were getting along with each other was terrible. At that time, the veterans were putting down the rookies. Everyone had a little clique. No one clique hung around with another. The players weren't communicating with each other. And of course, the talent level was much worse than the level it's at right now. The manager and some of the coaches who were there weren't really in control. All of them are gone now. That's been a major difference. There were problems.

But the organization has changed drastically, like going from day to night. In 1985, the ownership seemed to have the attitude that they would just throw a team out there and hope to break even financially. It seemed they weren't even considering winning. What a change there has been. Now it's, "We're going to put a team out there that can win. We're going to keep the players happy. And whatever happens, happens. But we're going to give it a shot."

This has been a great place to grow up in a baseball sense, especially considering you don't have a hectic lifestyle. If we lived in New York or Boston, places that are to me much faster, it would be harder to enjoy the kind of success we have had here. To me, the media is very overwhelming in those-type cities. I think the crowds there expect a lot out of you, and many times you're put in a situation where you can't win. One of the very positive things about being in the East Bay is the relative lack of pressure the players feel.

It's been an amazing ride, because with the free agent market open, you don't see teams keeping their players together anywhere else. This team has kept it together for two or three years and has a chance to keep it together for the next five or six with the contracts they've given to many of the key players. There are some young players who are going to be here and playing great for a long time like the Mark McGwires and the Walt Weisses. Also, most of the veterans should have four or five good years left. It seems that if those guys still want to play here, the front office would be happy to keep them here.

I see the front office having a commitment to make the magic last as long as it can. The players certainly see it that way. We acknowledge the fact that the organization has gone out of the way to keep the team together, to keep the players happy. They've really made a commitment to the fans of Oakland to put the best team in baseball on the field and to keep it together. They've put something special together. You don't often see a powerhouse in any sport these days.

We're not afraid of the word "dynasty." To me, the word is irrelevant. Fans or the media can say we're the worst team in baseball or they can say we're the best team in baseball or even the best team that's ever been assembled. It's not going to matter to us. Our attitude is not going to change. We're still going to work hard, we're still going to go out and play hard. Whatever they label us is not going to affect our performance level. We're going to go out and do the same things. That kind of attitude starts within each player. I think the manager can only do so much. The players are the ones who have to go out on the field and carry it off.

When I look at the whole package starting in 1988, the thing that sticks out the most for me is that the A's are a winning ballclub. We have the right attitude. We've had some tough times, and we've had some great times. Either way we've kept an even keel. We have stayed level mentally. One of the things that really impresses me is that every year we try to improve. We have had a great team at the start of each year, but as we need things, the front office will try to make improvements here and there as we go along. At times we've added starting pitching, an extra outfielder, and infield help. The front office is willing

to go out and make that kind of improvement just to make us that much stronger. And it's necessary, because other teams always will be trying to catch the A's.

There are two special memories I have of this time, one personal and one team-oriented. On a team level, what could be greater than winning the World Series that first time? We had so much adversity to overcome, but we had the players willing to make the sacrifices and the adjustments to do it. I missed half the year, but other guys picked up the slack and we kept on winning. That's the kind of drive it takes, and we had it. I'll never forget the feeling I had after we won Game 4 (of the World Series) in San Francisco.

On a personal level, nothing really compares with the season I had in 1988, winning the MVP trophy and becoming the first 40–40 man. I was never one to compare myself much with others, but it was special to do what nobody else had done. When I finally got that 40th stolen base (in Milwaukee in late September), there was a great sense of satisfaction and of a job accomplished. I think the best is still to come. From Jose Canseco and from the Oakland A's.

THIS PAGE: May 8, 1990, Oakland Coliseum. Jose Canseco eludes the tag of Rick Cerone in A's early season win over New York.

ABOVE: October 5, 1988, Fenway Park. Mark McGwire meets with the denizens of the sporting press after Oakland's first-game win in the playoffs against Boston.

A's punishing pitchers at Coliseum, 1990. THIS PAGE, RIGHT: Dennis Eckersley earning another save. BELOW: Mike Moore in the early evening of a Memorial Day. PAGE 73, TOP: Rick Honeycutt quelching a late-inning rally. PAGE 73, BOTTOM: Curt Young with rain falling.

Dennis Eckersley

For Dennis Eckersley, unparalleled success has come in the wake of his trade to Oakland in the spring of 1987.

It did not come without a price, however. Eckersley had been a starting pitcher his entire career and luxuriated in possessing one of the Cadillac jobs in baseball.

A's Pitching Coach Dave Duncan and Manager Tony La Russa saw him as a reliever, though, and, grudgingly at first, Eckersley made the switch. Within the space of a year, however, he'd become the best reliever in the game, averaging more than 40 saves from 1988 to 1990 and erasing Rollie Fingers' 136 saves as the Oakland career record.

For the Oakland-born and Fremont-raised Eckersley, the road to the Oakland bull pen took him through starting jobs in Cleveland, Boston and Chicago. With the Indians he was an All-Star five years after signing with them out of Fremont's Washington High. With the Red Sox he was a 20-game winner. With the Cubs he first tasted post-season success in 1984. It was not until his arrival in Oakland, however, that he emerged at the top of his profession.

For all of that, he says riding Oakland's post-season express, not rolling up great statistics and achieving personal success, is the most gratifying part of his Oakland career. After making it to the playoffs just once in his first 12 years in the majors, Eckersley, in his role as sure-fire closer, has become perhaps the single most important performer as the A's dynasty train has made three consecutive post-season stops.

■ To me, just being on a winner for the first time in my life for the last four years is the most important thing. I've never been on a team that was successful like this over this period of time. Ever. I've been on some good ball clubs, like the Red Sox who were primarily offensive-oriented ball clubs. This is the first ball club that really is based on pitching and defense because of the ball park we play in. And we happen to have some of the better young

talent, power-wise, in the league. So this is the most success I've ever had.

I've had a bunch of good years here because of the team I'm playing for. My success is based on the team's success, maybe more than anybody else on the team because of the way I've been used. I'm a good example of what they've done.

I resisted going from starter to relief, because it wasn't like I was going from starting to closing. I was in middle relief until Jay Howell got hurt. Even when I did a good job closing during the second half of 1987, I was the only one who knew next spring that I'd be the closer in

1988. It was my job, but I could have wasted it. Even at that point, if it was my choice, I'd still have been a starter because it's glorious, that job.

On the other hand, being a closer is a killer job. Now that I've had some more experience at it—luckily I've been successful—I've adapted. Back then, all it would have taken was for me to have a couple of bad outings, and I'd have had to say, "Hey, this job stinks, I'd like to starter again." That was a long time ago, though. Even when I was young and had success with Cleveland and Boston, things were never like this. I never got the attention then that I do now—not even close. It's all because of winning. Winning is it. Now I can see that this is a glorious job when you win, no getting around it.

But the thing that many people don't realize is that whatever I do in terms of numbers, it is because of the opportunities that other guys have given me. The middle relievers—Geno (Gene Nelson), Honey (Rick Honeycutt) and Burnsie (Todd Burns)—have been unbelievable the last three years. If they have trouble, then I'm not going to be saving many games, because I need them to set the table. And the thing is, the A's showed they realized that by signing Geno and Honey to contract extensions. The front office doesn't want to let something special go, and, face it, what we have here is very, very unique.

Sometimes when I look back and see the numbers I put up, I don't know what to think. I've never really been wrapped up in numbers. And I've never really cared about being the best. All I ever wanted was to be a guy who was as good as he could be. If that makes me the best, fine. If not, that's OK, too.

When I first came here, playing at home was very special to me. But the meaning has changed for me in the last year or two. What it means now is that I'm comfortable. The Bay Area is not like any other place. Everything is so familiar, and that's nice. It's just a great place to play, regardless of whether or not I come from here. The fans aren't so harsh here. It's a nice atmosphere, being as I come from here.

I guess the longer I stay here, the more it seems like I've been here my whole career. It's four years now, and it seems like I've been here for 10. So that the feeling of coming back home is gone. Because this *is* home.

We're very professional as a club. We're not forcing rah-rah-rah stuff on anyone. The player-to-player and player-to-manager respect factor is there. This club gets along better than any club I've ever been on. Very easily. It's not like we all go out and pal around together, but we get along so well, it's kind of boring—the best kind of boring.

We have a job to do here. It's not like we're all shocked at where we're standing right now. We've worked hard to get to where we are, and when we go on the field, we expect to win. You know you won't win all of the time, but you expect to, and when we don't it's like, bummer. It really is. Others accept losing. We don't. We don't ever want to get a feeling for it.

RIGHT: March 1989, Chandler, Arizona. Tony La Russa surveys his troops early in the first spring game. BELOW: October 20, 1988, Oakland Coliseum. Moments after the Dodgers beat the A's in the fifth and final game of the World Series, Dave Stewart congratulates Bob Welch in the quiet of the A's clubhouse, saying "We've had a great season. We've got nothing to be ashamed of."

ABOVE: October 6, 1989, SkyDome, Toronto. Mike Gallego turns a double play, but A's bow to Blue Jays, 6-5, in Game 3 of the ALCS. LEFT: March 13, 1989, Phoenix, Arizona. General manager Sandy Alderson watches the ball club work out in spring training.

RIGHT: October 28, 1989, Candlestick Park, San Francisco. Commissioner Fay Vincent presents the World Championship trophy to A's owner Walter Haas as his son and club president, Wally Haas, A's general manager Sandy Alderson, and American League president Bobby Brown look on. BELOW: October 6, 1989, SkyDome, Toronto. Flanked by general manager Sandy Alderson (left) and A's executive Bill Rigney (right), the Haas family prepares to watch the A's battle the Toronto Blue Jays. PAGE 79, TOP: October 17, 1989, Candlestick Park, San Francisco. Moments after the great earthquake, Fay Vincent, his mouth open in wonderment, stares out onto the playing field. PAGE 79, BOTTOM: October 27, 1989. A's dugout moments before taking the field at Candlestick Park to resume earthquake-delayed Game 3 of the 1989 World Series.

ABOVE: October 15, 1989, Oakland Coliseum. Terry Steinbach scores as A's thump Giants in the second game of the World Series. RIGHT: October 8, 1989, SkyDome, Toronto. With champagne flying, Rickey Henderson holds the MVP trophy for the American League Championship Series. PAGE 81: October 6, 1990, Fenway Park, Boston. Dennis Eckersley receives postgame congrats from teammates after saving the first game of the ALCS against the Red Sox.

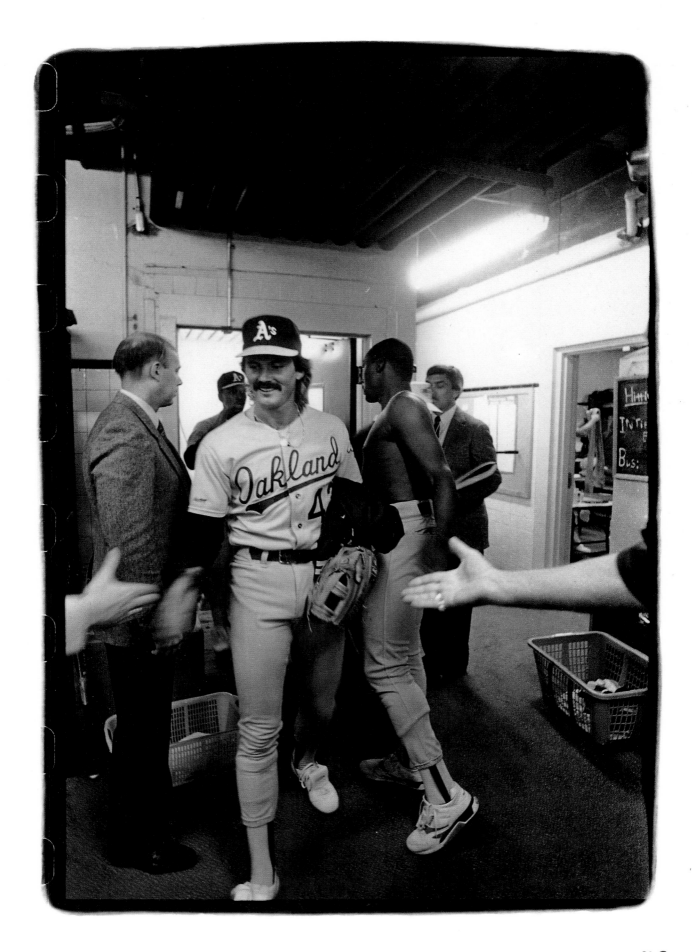

ABOVE: October 16, 1990, Riverfront Stadium, Cincinnati. National anthem.
PAGE 82: October 7, 1990, Fenway Park, Boston. Walt Weiss injures his knee and
is lost to the Athletics for the remainder of the year in A's 4-1 win over the Red
Sox in ALCS Game 2.

RIGHT: October 16, 1990, Riverfront Stadium, Cincinnati. Willie McGee limbers up before taking the field in Game 1 of the World Series. BELOW: October 7, 1990, Fenway Park, Boston. Larry Davis stretches Bob Welch in the A's clubhouse prior to the A's second-game win over the Red Sox. PAGE 85: October 17, 1990, Riverfront Stadium, Cincinnati. Rickey Henderson robs Todd Benziger of extra bases with a circus catch late in the second game of the World Series.

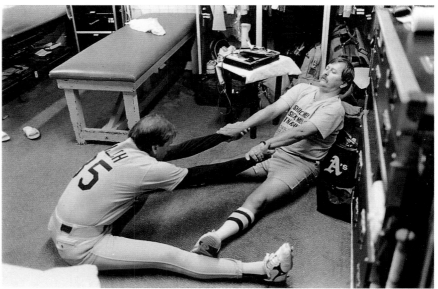

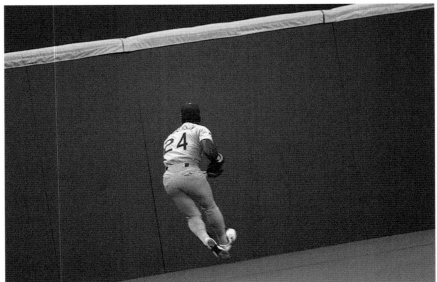

RIGHT: October 16, 1990, Riverfront Stadium, Cincinnati. Terry Steinbach reaches for an errant throw as Barry Larkin scores in Cincinnati's 7-0 win in Game 1 of the World Series. BELOW: October 7, 1990, Fenway Park, Boston. Bob Welch pitches Athletics past Boston to win Game 2 of the ALCS. PAGE 87, ABOVE: October 19, 1990, Oakland Coliseum. Harold Baines belts a home run to give Oakland an early lead in Game 3 of the World Series. PAGE 87, BELOW: October 17, 1990, Riverfront Stadium, Cincinnati. Former teammates Jose Rijo and Dave Stewart share a moment of light banter before the start of Game 2 of the World Series.